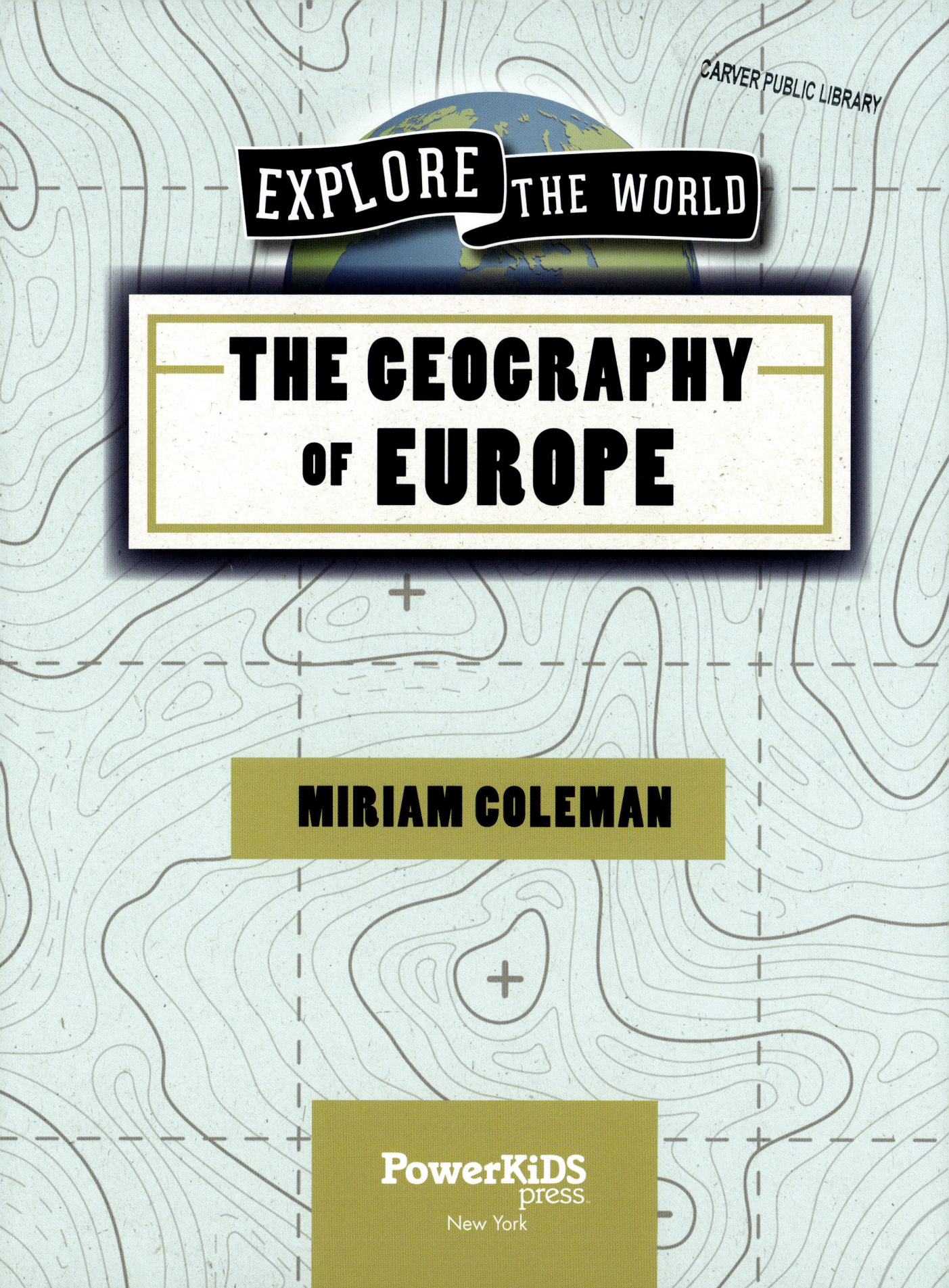

Published in 2021 by The Rosen Publishing Group, Inc.
29 East 21st Street, New York, NY 10010

Copyright © 2021 by The Rosen Publishing Group, Inc.

All rights reserved. No part of this book may be reproduced in any form without permission in writing from the publisher, except by a reviewer.

First Edition

Editor: Caitie McAneney
Book Design: Tanya Dellaccio

Photo Credits: Cover mikroman6/Moment/Getty Images; series background MicroOne/ Getty Images; p. 5 (top) Adisa/Shutterstock.com; p. 5 (bottom) Dmitry Rukhlenko/Shutterstock.com; p. 7 Vladislav Gurfinkel/Shutterstock.com; p. 9 Olga Gavrilova/Shutterstock.com; p. 11 Daniele Sartori/Moment/ Getty Images; p. 12 Bardocz Peter/Shutterstock.com; p. 13 Danita Delimont/Gallo Images/Getty Images Plus; p. 15 (top) Jorisvo/iStock/Getty Images Plus; p. 15 (bottom) Westend61/Getty Images; p. 17 Christian Fitt/Shutterstock.com; p. 19 (top) stockcam/iStock/Getty Images Plus; p. 19 (bottom) BERTRAND LANGLOIS/AFP Creative/Getty Images Plus; p.20 https://upload.wikimedia.org/wikipedia/commons/5/53/MODIS_-_Great_Britain_and_Ireland_-_2012-06-04_during_heat_wave.jpg; p. 21 Aping Vision/STS/Photographer's Choice/Getty Images Plus; p. 23 (top) S.Borisov/Shutterstock.com; p. 23 (bottom) S-F/Shutterstock.com; p. 25 Sven Hansche/Shutterstock.com; p. 27 RelaxFoto.de/E+/Getty Images; p. 28 Daniele COSSU/Shutterstock.com; p. 29 Liv Oeian/Shutterstock.com.

Cataloging-in-Publication Data
Names: Coleman, Miriam.
Title: The geography of Europe / Miriam Coleman.
Description: New York : PowerKids Press, 2021. | Series: Explore the world | Includes glossary and index.
Identifiers: ISBN 9781725321960 (pbk.) | ISBN 9781725321984 (library bound) | ISBN 9781725321977 (6 pack) | ISBN 9781725321991 (ebook)
Subjects: LCSH: Europe–Juvenile literature. | Europe–Geography–Juvenile literature.
Classification: LCC D1051.C563 2021 | DDC 940–dc23

Manufactured in the United States of America

CPSIA Compliance Information: Batch #CSPK20: For Further Information contact Rosen Publishing, New York, New York at 1-800-237-9932

CONTENTS

A LAND OF CONTRASTS 4
PENINSULA OF PENINSULAS 6
THE LAY OF THE LAND 8
TOWERING MOUNTAINS 10
COASTAL EUROPE 12
A CONTINENT UNITED 14
SHIFTING PEOPLES 16
RIDING THE RAILS 18
SPOTLIGHT ON LONDON 20
POSTCARD FROM PARIS 22
WHERE ANCIENT AND MODERN WORLDS MEET . . 24
CLIMATE CHANGE 26
THE SPIRIT OF COOPERATION 28
GLOSSARY 30
FOR MORE INFORMATION 31
INDEX 32

A LAND OF CONTRASTS

Europe is the second-smallest continent in the world, taking up barely one-fifteenth of the planet's land mass. Yet this relatively small space holds a world of contrasts and about 50 independent nations. Europe is home to very different climates, from the warm Mediterranean region to the frozen Arctic North. More than 60 different languages are **indigenous** to Europe, and immigrant populations from around the world bring even more.

With all its differences, however, Europe has a distinctive culture. Geographical factors like wide-open spaces and a dense transportation network bring the continent together and allow people and information to flow across borders. Despite the long history of war between nations in Europe, recent decades have seen peace and cooperation.

NOT QUITE A CONTINENT

Although we know Europe as one of the world's seven continents, it is actually a part of the supercontinent of Eurasia, which also includes Asia. To be a true continent, Europe would need to be surrounded by water on all sides. Although there is some debate over Europe's borders, the Ural Mountains, the Ural River, and the Black and Caspian Seas are usually considered the boundary between Europe and Asia. Russia and Turkey are both transcontinental nations, with land in both continents.

These photographs of Greece (above) and Norway (below) show just how different the geography and climates of Europe can be.

THINK LIKE A GEOGRAPHER

EUROPE AND ASIA BOTH SIT ON THE SAME TECTONIC PLATE, CALLED THE EURASIAN PLATE.

PENINSULA OF PENINSULAS

Europe lies at the western end of Eurasia. Most of Europe is a **peninsula** of Eurasia. Its bordering waters are the Atlantic Ocean to the west, the Arctic Ocean to the north, and the Mediterranean, the Black, and the Caspian Seas in the south. The greater peninsula of Europe is actually made up of smaller peninsulas that extend out from the main body of Europe: the Iberian, the Italian (or Apennine), and the Balkan Peninsulas in the south, and the Scandinavian and the Jutland Peninsulas in the north.

Europe also includes many islands off the coast of its mainland. These include the British Isles, Iceland, the southern islands of Greece and Malta, and Norway's Svalbard **archipelago**, near the North Pole.

THINK LIKE A GEOGRAPHER

EUROPE'S CLOSEST POINT TO AFRICA COMES AT THE STRAIT OF GIBRALTAR, A CHANNEL OF WATER THAT CONNECTS THE MEDITERRANEAN SEA TO THE ATLANTIC OCEAN. AT THE STRAIT'S NARROWEST POINT, THE DISTANCE BETWEEN SPAIN, IN EUROPE, AND MOROCCO, IN AFRICA, IS 8 MILES (12.9 KM).

PENINSULA: A PIECE OF LAND THAT IS CONNECTED TO A MAINLAND AND IS SURROUNDED ON THREE SIDES BY WATER.

WORLD'S LARGEST ISLAND

The world's largest island is a part of Europe—sort of. Greenland, which lies in the northern Atlantic Ocean, is part of the Kingdom of Denmark, although it is much closer to North America. It even shares geographical structures, such as the **Canadian Shield**, with North America. In fact, it is only 16 miles (25.7 km) from Canada's Ellesmere Island, while its nearest European neighbor, Iceland, is around 200 miles (321.9 km) away. Despite being part of the Danish kingdom, Greenland's population of around 57,000 people has a home-rule government, or is self-governing.

This satellite image of Europe shows the shape of the land, made up of many peninsulas reaching out into the sea.

CANADIAN SHIELD: THE PLATEAU REGION OF EASTERN CANADA AND THE NORTHEASTERN UNITED STATES, MAKING UP THE LARGEST MASS OF EXPOSED PRECAMBRIAN ROCK ON EARTH.

THE LAY OF THE LAND

The largest landform in Europe is the Great European Plain, a huge area of flat land that sprawls across the continent. It stretches from the foot of the Pyrenees Mountains in France to the Ural Mountains in Russia. It is one of the biggest areas of uninterrupted flat land in the world, and it provided the settlers of Europe with many advantages, including farming and trade, as they built their societies. The section of this plain that extends through France, Belgium, the Netherlands, Scandinavia, northern Germany, and Poland is known as the North European Plain.

The North European Plain was once covered in thick forests of oak, elm, ash, linden, and maple trees. In the Middle Ages, people began clearing much of the land to build villages and fields. Only a small portion of the great forests remains today.

GLACIAL SCULPTING

The landscapes of the Scandinavian countries Norway, Sweden, and Denmark have their own distinctive features. A part of the geographic formation called the Western Uplands, this region has been shaped by the movement of ancient glaciers. As the glaciers retreated from the area after the last ice age, they left behind deep valleys carved into the rock surface. These valleys then filled with seawater and became fjords, or steep-sided inlets connected to the sea. Norway is famous for the beauty of its fjords.

ICE AGE: A TIME PERIOD WHEN GLACIERS ARE WIDESPREAD ON EARTH.

This view of Lysefjord in Norway shows how dramatically ancient glaciers shaped the land.

THINK LIKE A GEOGRAPHER

THE NORTH EUROPEAN PLAIN IS THE MOST DENSELY POPULATED REGION OF EUROPE.

TOWERING MOUNTAINS

Although much of Europe's landscape is characterized by flat plains, it has its share of majestic mountain peaks as well. The highest, most rugged of these mountains rise up from the Alpine mountain system. This system cuts across the middle of the continent and divides central and southern Europe.

The most famous range of mountains in this system is the Alps, which stretch for 750 miles (1,207 km) across Albania, Austria, Bosnia and Herzegovina, Croatia, France, Germany, Italy, Montenegro, Serbia, Slovenia, and Switzerland. Many of Europe's important rivers—including the Rhine, the Danube, the Po, and the Rhône—have their source in the Alps. The natural beauty of this region, along with the development of holiday resorts, has made the Alps a major tourist destination for skiing and hiking. This, unfortunately, has threatened the mountains' sensitive ecosystem.

THINK LIKE A GEOGRAPHER

THE ALPINE REGION ALSO INCLUDES THE PYRENEES, THE APENNINES, THE DINARIC ALPS, AND THE CARPATHIAN MOUNTAINS.

Mont Blanc stands nearly 16,000 feet (4,876.8 m) above sea level on the border between France and Italy. It is the tallest peak in the Alps.

FIERY ERUPTIONS

Amid the peaks of the Alpine mountain region lie a number of deadly, active volcanoes. Mount Vesuvius, on the Bay of Naples in southern Italy, erupted in AD 79. It completely buried several ancient Roman cities, including Pompeii and Herculaneum. Although Mount Vesuvius is still active, nearly 600,000 people live just 6.2 miles (10 km) from it, in the dangerous "red zone." The highest active volcano in Europe is Mount Etna, on the Italian island of Sicily. It stands 10,810 feet (3,294.9 m) high.

COASTAL EUROPE

With its many peninsulas and islands, Europe has about 42,250 miles (67,994.8 km) of coastline. From its sunny Mediterranean beaches in the south to the deepwater ports on the North Sea, Europe's coasts influence what its people eat, how they make their living, and how they communicate with the rest of the world.

The waters around Europe are divided into four sea regions: the Mediterranean Sea, the Black Sea, the Baltic Sea, and the North-East Atlantic Ocean, which includes the Arctic, the North, the Barents, the Irish and Celtic Seas, the Bay of Biscay, and the Iberian Coast. The Mediterranean Sea has the most **diversity** in terms of living things, while the continent's most valuable fishing areas as well as its largest oil and gas reserves are found in the North-East Atlantic.

This map shows the major sea regions of Europe.

INLAND WATERWAYS

The rivers that flow through Europe provide vital links between countries, transportation throughout the continent, and important **watersheds** for cities and agriculture. Many of Europe's cities, including Paris, London, and Budapest, were built along the banks of rivers. The Danube is Europe's longest river outside of Russia, flowing for 1,780 miles (2,864.6 km) through 10 different countries. Its source is in western Germany's Black Forest mountain range and it passes through cities such as Vienna, Budapest, and Belgrade before emptying out into the Black Sea.

The Danube River flows through several European capital cities, including Budapest, Hungary.

THINK LIKE A GEOGRAPHER

EUROPE'S LARGEST PORT IS IN ROTTERDAM, IN THE NETHERLANDS. ROTTERDAM, WHICH IS LINKED BY A CANAL TO THE NORTH SEA, IS ONE OF THE BUSIEST SHIPPING PORTS IN THE WORLD.

DIVERSITY: EXHIBITING A VARIETY OF TYPES.

A CONTINENT UNITED

Europe has been plagued by wars throughout its history. In 1958, after the horrors of World War II, six countries joined together to create a **supranational organization**. The European Economic Community, as the organization was first called, originally focused on helping countries trade with each other so that they were less likely to fight. More countries soon joined in, and in 1993, the organization became a political body called the European Union (EU).

The 27 countries that have joined the EU are called members. The members have agreed to a common set of laws concerning issues such as human rights, environmental regulations, and security. The citizens of EU countries have the right to live, work, and travel in any member states.

THINK LIKE A GEOGRAPHER

IN 1999, MOST MEMBERS OF THE EUROPEAN UNION REPLACED THEIR OWN LOCAL **CURRENCIES** WITH A COMMON MONETARY UNIT CALLED THE EURO. THE GROUP OF NATIONS THAT USE THIS CURRENCY MAKES UP THE EUROZONE.

SUPRANATIONAL ORGANIZATION: A COLLECTION OF MULTIPLE STATES THAT MAKE UP A LARGER GROUP THAT GOES BEYOND NATIONAL BOUNDARIES.

EUROPE'S CAPITAL?

Although the European Union does not have an official capital city, the city of Brussels in Belgium is the organization's **administrative** center. Brussels is host to most of the EU's important institutions, including the European Commission, the European Council, and the European Parliament. Brussels's central location and access to transportation options like high-speed trains have made the Belgian city a practical choice for this work, although some other EU institutions are based in Strasbourg, France, and the **microstate** of Luxembourg.

MICROSTATE: A NATION THAT IS EXTREMELY SMALL IN AREA AND POPULATION.

Flags of the European Union wave outside the EU Parliament building in Brussels, Belgium.

EUROPEAN UNION PARLIAMENT BUILDING

SHIFTING PEOPLES

For many decades, the countries of western Europe have enjoyed a high **standard of living** compared to their neighbors to the east. With a relatively mild **maritime** climate that was good for agriculture, the western part of the continent had many advantages from its earliest days of settlement. Beginning in the mid-19th century, England, Germany, the Netherlands, Belgium, and northern France also became major industrial centers and important producers of coal, steel, and chemicals.

Since citizens of the European Union can live and work anywhere within the supranational organization, many people from eastern European countries, such as Poland and Romania, **migrate** to western countries, such as France and England, to find jobs. The competition for jobs in these regions has led to tension between locals and newcomers seeking work.

THE CHANGING FACE OF EUROPE

Migration often brings change to the cultural landscape. It may eventually alter the character of a place, or the political, economic, social, and cultural characteristics that make each city or country unique. In Europe, the migration of people from North Africa and southwest Asia (often from former European colonies) has brought diversity to traditionally Christian or **secular** communities. The building of Islamic **mosques**, as well as cultural practices, such as wearing the **hijab**, have led to clashes between cultural communities.

One of the largest mosques in Europe, Germany's Cologne Central Mosque can hold up to 1,200 people for prayers in its main hall.

STANDARD OF LIVING: THE AMOUNT OF WEALTH AND PURCHASING POWER OF A PARTICULAR GROUP.

MIGRATE: TO MOVE FROM ONE REGION TO ANOTHER.

THINK LIKE A GEOGRAPHER

THE LARGEST MOSQUE IN GERMANY, THE COLOGNE CENTRAL MOSQUE, DREW CONTROVERSY WHEN IT OPENED IN 2017 IN A CITY MOST FAMOUS FOR ITS CATHOLIC CATHEDRAL. YET MOSQUES HAVE ACTUALLY BEEN A PART OF THE EUROPEAN LANDSCAPE FOR WELL OVER 1,000 YEARS.

RIDING THE RAILS

One major way people and goods move between Europe's cities and countries is through the continent's remarkable network of railroads.

In 1825, Britain built the first public railway for steam locomotives, connecting the northeastern industrial towns of Stockton and Darlington. The railroads soon expanded, moving resources like iron and coal from the north to factories in cities across the country. Trains also allowed people to travel more easily to find jobs.

Around the same time, railways took hold on Europe's mainland, beginning with France, Belgium, and Germany. By the turn of the 20th century, these railroads connected all the countries of continental Europe, eventually growing to form **transportation corridors** that cross the continent on various routes from north to south and east to west.

RIVERS AND ROADS

Long before railroads crisscrossed the continent, Europeans moved goods and people along rivers. By the Middle Ages, inland waterways like the Rhine River had become a major mode of transportation. Over time, people altered the natural water bodies by dredging to make them deeper, calming their rapids, building locks, and digging canals to connect rivers to each other. The roads and highways that make up another essential link in Europe's transportation corridors also have ancient roots. The Romans began building their first highway, the Appian Way, in 312 BC.

TRANSPORTATION CORRIDOR: AN AREA OF LAND THAT INCLUDES LINES OF TRANSPORTATION, LIKE RAILROADS, HIGHWAYS, AND CANALS.

With trains providing connections all across the continent, busy railway stations like the Gare du Nord in Paris are distinctive features of European cities.

THINK LIKE A GEOGRAPHER

IN 1994, THE TWO BRANCHES OF THE EUROPEAN RAIL NETWORK WERE JOINED BY THE OPENING OF THE CHANNEL TUNNEL, A 31-MILE (49.9 KM) RAIL TUNNEL RUNNING UNDER THE ENGLISH CHANNEL BETWEEN FRANCE AND ENGLAND.

SPOTLIGHT ON LONDON

The capital of both England and the United Kingdom is London. The city is located in the southeast region of England along the River Thames. Greater London has a population of over 9 million people, and it is both the United Kingdom's largest city and its most diverse, with its residents speaking more than 300 different languages and representing many **ethnicities**. London also has a large immigrant population, with more than 37 percent coming from other countries.

The Thames flows 215 miles (346 km) from its source in the Cotswold Hills to its mouth on the North Sea. It has long provided an important connection between London, the interior of England, and the rest of the world.

THE BRITISH ISLES

The British Isles are an archipelago in the North Atlantic Ocean. The two largest islands in this group are the nations of Ireland and Great Britain. Great Britain is home to the countries of England, Scotland, and Wales. These countries, together with Northern Ireland, make up the **sovereign** state called the United Kingdom. The British Isles also consist of thousands of smaller islands, including the Isle of Man, the Hebrides, and the Shetland Islands.

ETHNICITY: A GROUP THAT SHARES COMMON CULTURAL TRAITS, SUCH AS LANGUAGE.

THINK LIKE A GEOGRAPHER

London is home to the world's oldest subway system. The London Underground, which first opened in 1863, now handles up to 5 million passenger trips a day.

The Houses of Parliament, seat of government of the United Kingdom, are located on the River Thames in London.

POSTCARD FROM PARIS

France's capital, Paris, is nicknamed "the City of Light." It is widely regarded as one of the most beautiful cities in the world. Paris is located in north-central France, in a region known as the Paris Basin. Thanks to its rich soil and network of rivers, the Paris Basin is France's main agricultural region. The city of Paris itself is famous for its wonderful food, from rich pastries like éclairs and croissants, to fancy meals in its many restaurants. Paris is also known worldwide as a center for art and literature.

The tree-lined Seine River snakes through the center of the city. The forests of beech and oak trees that surround the city are called the "lungs of Paris" because they help keep the air clean.

DIVERSE LANDSCAPES

France is the largest country in western Europe, and its borders contain many of the contrasting climates and landscapes that make the rest of the continent so diverse. The busy beaches of the French Riviera lie on the warm Mediterranean coast, while the Bay of Biscay on the Atlantic Ocean offers a wilder, rougher coastline. The fertile plains of the north and west of the country make France an agricultural powerhouse, while the French Alps and the Pyrenees mountain range provide habitats for wildlife.

The Eiffel Tower rises over the Seine River in Paris.

THINK LIKE A GEOGRAPHER

Paris's most famous monument is the Eiffel Tower. Built by Gustave Eiffel for the 1889 World's Fair, the tower stands nearly 1,000 feet (304.8 m) tall and was the tallest structure in the world until 1930.

WHERE ANCIENT AND MODERN WORLDS MEET

Athens is the capital of Greece and one of the world's oldest cities. It is known as the birthplace of Western civilization. Athens was first settled more than 7,000 years ago, and people have lived there ever since. The city is filled with monuments of its ancient past, yet it is a crowded modern city as well. It has a subway and trolley system, apartment buildings, luxury hotels, and several large sports stadiums built for the 2004 Olympics.

The heart of Athens is the Acropolis, which sits on a flat limestone hill high above the city. One of the city's earliest settlements, the Acropolis was founded around 5000 BC. It holds some of Greece's most important ancient monuments, including a famous fifth-century Greek temple called the Parthenon.

A SEAFARING NATION

Greece lies at the southern tip of the Balkan Peninsula. The country includes more than 2,000 islands spreading into the Aegean, the Ionian, and the Mediterranean Seas. Rugged mountain terrain cuts off the country from mainland Europe to the north, so the Greeks have relied on travel by sea for thousands of years. Shipping remains one of the biggest parts of the Greek economy, and Greece is the top ship-owning nation in the world.

THINK LIKE A GEOGRAPHER

ATHENS IS THE SOUTHERNMOST CAPITAL CITY OF MAINLAND EUROPE. VALLETTA, THE CAPITAL OF THE ISLAND NATION OF MALTA, IS EVEN FARTHER SOUTH.

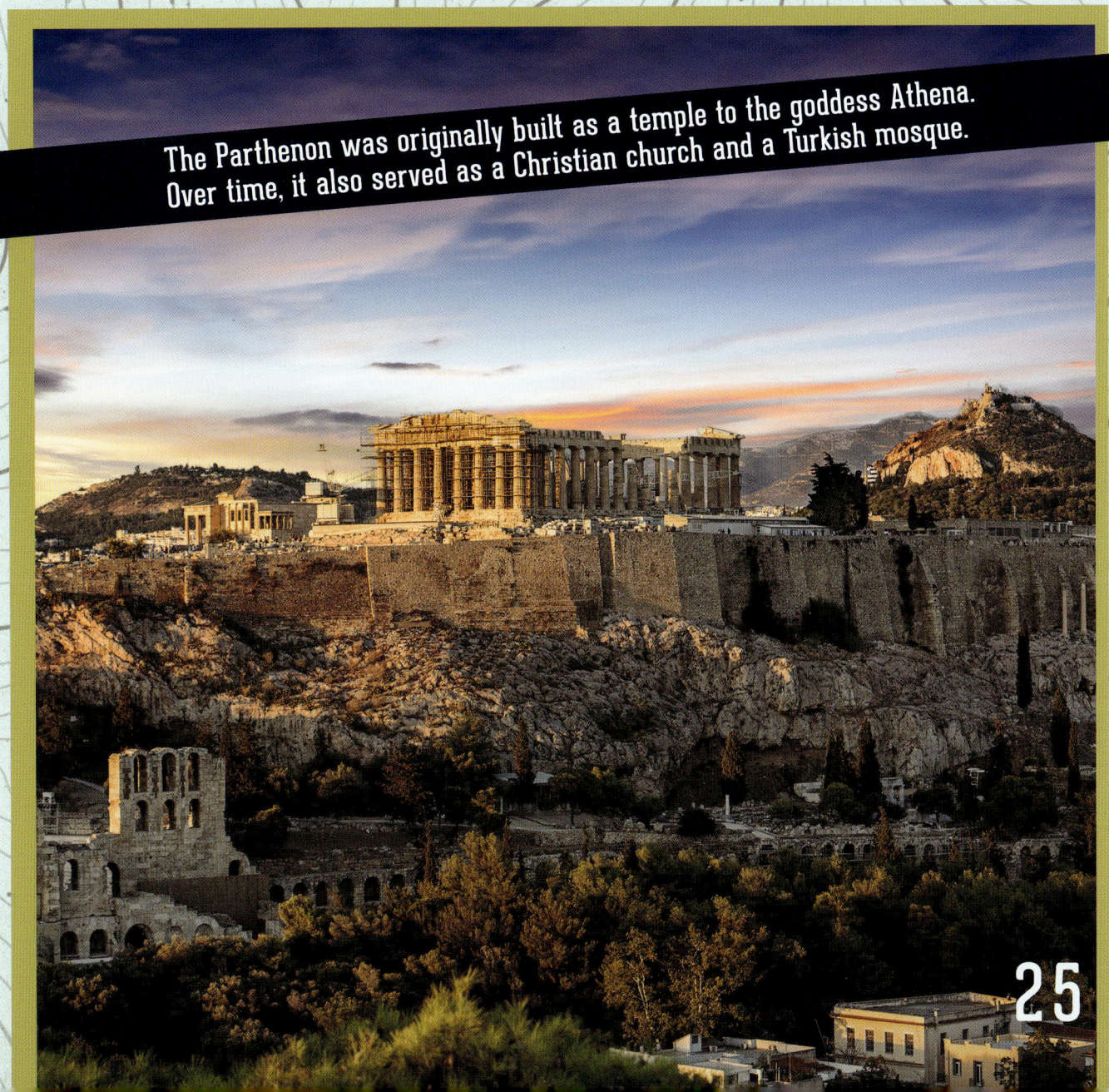

The Parthenon was originally built as a temple to the goddess Athena. Over time, it also served as a Christian church and a Turkish mosque.

CLIMATE CHANGE

For thousands of years, Europeans have been changing the land to suit their needs. They have cleared forests to build their villages and cities, drained marshland to grow their fields, and dug tunnels through the Alps to aid their travel.

Yet in recent decades, the impact of human development on Europe's environment has resulted in many worrying changes. Global temperatures have risen from increased greenhouse gases in the atmosphere. At the same time, record-breaking heat waves have swept across Europe. In countries with temperate climates, like France and the United Kingdom, this has disrupted farming and set off dangerous wildfires. Countries near the Arctic Ocean witness sea ice melting at an alarming rate. This leads to ocean levels rising everywhere, and low-lying cities like Venice, Italy, are in danger of sinking into the sea.

THINK LIKE A GEOGRAPHER

THE EUROPEAN UNION IS THE THIRD-LARGEST GREENHOUSE GAS EMITTER IN THE WORLD, AFTER CHINA AND THE UNITED STATES.

RISING SEA LEVELS

The Netherlands borders the North Sea and occupies some of the lowest land in Europe. Rising sea levels due to climate change are a major threat to this country. After hundreds of years fighting against floods by building dams and **dikes**, the Dutch (the people of the Netherlands) came up with a new approach. Instead of trying to keep water out of their land, they are building lakes, parks, and even parking garages that can serve as **reservoirs** to hold water when the seas and rivers overflow.

As climate change causes sea levels to rise, low-lying cities like Venice, Italy, face more frequent and severe flooding.

THE SPIRIT OF COOPERATION

Europe faces many challenges in the future, from shifting populations to natural disasters brought on by global warming. These challenges will affect the continent's different regions in different ways. But the spirit of unity and cooperation promoted by the European Union aims to provide a pathway for the whole continent to find solutions together.

The EU has been especially active in crafting laws to address climate change. In addition to creating programs to reduce its greenhouse gas emissions, the EU aims to make the continent more **resilient** in the face of a changing climate, and to encourage its people and governments to live in a way that is more sustainable.

GRETA THUNBERG, CLIMATE ACTIVIST

Young people in Europe have taken the reins in fighting to protect the planet. Among the strongest voices in the fight against climate change has been a Swedish teenager named Greta Thunberg, founder of a movement called Fridays for Future. Starting with small weekly protests outside the Swedish Parliament, Thunberg has drawn millions of other young people across the world into her school strike, addressing world leaders and demanding action.

THINK LIKE A GEOGRAPHER

IN 2012, THE EUROPEAN UNION WAS AWARDED THE NOBEL PEACE PRIZE FOR HELPING TO "TRANSFORM MOST OF EUROPE FROM A CONTINENT OF WAR TO A CONTINENT OF PEACE."

"We showed that we are united and that we, young people, are unstoppable," climate activist Greta Thunberg said in an address to the United Nations Youth Climate Summit in September 2019.

GLOSSARY

administrative: Having to do with the part of a government that manages the running of a certain area.

archipelago: A group of islands.

currency: A system of money in use in a particular country.

dike: A long wall or embankment built to prevent flooding from the sea.

hijab: The traditional covering for the hair and neck that is worn by Muslim women.

indigenous: Describing groups that are native to a particular region.

maritime: Relating to the sea or sailing.

mosque: A building that is used for Muslim religious services.

reservoir: A usually manmade lake where water is stored.

resilient: Able to recover from difficult conditions.

secular: Not religious.

sovereign: Having independent authority and the right to govern itself.

tectonic plate: One of the moveable masses of rock that create Earth's surface.

watershed: An area of land whose water drains into a particular river or waterway.

FOR MORE INFORMATION

BOOKS

Knufinke, Joana Costa. *Europe*. New York, NY: Scholastic, Inc., 2019.

Rockett, Paul. *Mapping Europe*. New York, NY: Crabtree Publishing Company, 2016.

Watson, Danielle. *The City in Medieval Europe*. New York, NY: Cavendish Square Publishing, 2017.

WEBSITES

European Union Learning Corner
europa.eu/learning-corner/
Play games and explore activities to learn about the European Union.

France Facts
www.natgeokids.com/uk/discover/geography/countries/facts-about-france/
Find out more about France, a European country with diverse geographical features!

National Geographic Kids: Countries
kids.nationalgeographic.com/explore/countries/
Explore different countries with slideshows, facts, and maps.

Publisher's note to educators and parents: Our editors have carefully reviewed these websites to ensure that they are suitable for students. Many websites change frequently, however, and we cannot guarantee that a site's future contents will continue to meet our high standards of quality and educational value. Be advised that students should be closely supervised whenever they access the internet.

INDEX

A
agriculture, 13, 16, 22

B
borders, 4, 6, 11, 22, 27

C
cities, 13, 15, 17, 19, 20, 21, 22, 23, 24, 25, 26, 27

climate, 4, 5, 16, 22, 26

climate change, 26, 27, 28

E
Eurasia, 4, 6

European Union (EU), 14, 15, 16, 26, 28, 29

F
fjords, 8, 9

forests, 8, 22, 26

G
glaciers, 8, 9

I
immigrants, 4, 20

islands, 6, 7, 11, 12, 20, 24, 25

L
languages, 4, 20

M
migration, 16

mountains, 4, 8, 10, 11, 13, 22, 24

O
oceans, 6, 7, 12, 20, 22, 26

P
peninsulas, 6, 12, 24

plains, 8, 9, 22

R
resources, 12, 18

rivers, 4, 10, 13, 18, 20, 21, 22, 23, 27

S
seas, 4, 6, 8, 12, 13, 20, 24, 26, 27

T
Thunberg, Greta, 28, 29

transportation, 4, 13, 15, 18, 19, 21, 24

V
volcanoes, 11